C000215293

THE BEAUTY OF CONFESSION WITH POPE FRANCIS

Discovering God's Mercy

by
Fr Donncha Ó hAodha

*All booklets are published thanks to the
generous support of the members of the
Catholic Truth Society*

CATHOLIC TRUTH SOCIETY
PUBLISHERS TO THE HOLY SEE

Contents

All rights reserved. First published 2016 by The Incorporated Catholic Truth Society, 40-46 Harleyford Road London SE11 5AY Tel: 020 7640 0042 Fax: 020 7640 0046. © 2016 The Incorporated Catholic Truth Society.

ISBN 978 1 78469 107 3

The Call to Confession

A truly worthwhile challenge

Do not be afraid of confession! When one is in line to go to confession, one feels all these things, even shame, but then when one finishes confession one leaves free, grand, beautiful, forgiven, candid, happy. This is the beauty of confession! I would like to ask you - but don't say it aloud, everyone respond in his heart: when was the last time you made your confession? Everyone think about it… Two days, two weeks, two years, twenty years, forty years? Everyone count, everyone say "when was the last time I went to confession?" And if much time has passed, do not lose another day. Go, the priest will be good. Jesus is there, and Jesus is more benevolent than priests, Jesus receives you, he receives you with so much love. Be courageous and go to confession![1]

These words of Pope Francis can be a helpful challenge to all of us. Perhaps we are thinking about going to confession again after a long time. Perhaps we receive this sacrament from time to time but are considering going more often. Maybe we go regularly but would like to deepen our knowledge and appreciation of the sacrament of penance.

We may also be seeking ways of explaining confession better to others. Taking up Francis's invitation to be "instruments of mercy" we may be trying, notwithstanding our own sinfulness and frailty, to encourage others to discover or rediscover this great sacrament of divine mercy.

The Holy Father's abundant preaching on the sacrament of forgiveness is a call to conversion addressed to all of us. It is also a catechesis on confession which addresses many of the questions we may have. Why do we need confession in the first place? What is the place of this sacrament in the Christian life? Are we truly forgiven? Why confess to a priest and not directly to God? How do we overcome feelings of unworthiness and shame? How often should one go to confession? What are effects of receiving this sacrament? How does sacramental reconciliation help us in our relationship with others? How does this sacrament affect the life of the Church?

Recent popes on this sacrament

The beauty of the sacrament of confession is a key teaching of Pope Francis. From the very start of his pontificate the Holy Father has emphasised the immense mercy of God. A few days after his election the Pope celebrated Mass in the Parish of St Anne at the Vatican. There he said those words which he has since repeated often in this preaching: "The Lord never tires of forgiving: never! It is we who tire of asking his forgiveness".[2]

Francis's emphasis on the necessity of confession is in total continuity with the teaching of his predecessors. St John Paul II tirelessly encouraged a renewed appreciation and promotion of this sacrament. His second encyclical *Dives in Misericordia* (30th November 1980) is a profound meditation on the Father who is "rich in mercy" (*Ep* 2:4), while his Apostolic Exhortation *Reconciliatio et Paenitentia* (2nd December 1984) is a comprehensive teaching "on Reconciliation and Penance in the Mission of the Church today" which has lost nothing of its timeliness. St John Paul II decided that the first saint to be canonised during the Great Jubilee of the Year 2000 would be Sr Mary Faustina Kowalska, an outstanding modern apostle of divine mercy. During the canonisation ceremony, the Holy Father instituted the second Sunday of Easter (or *Dominica in albis*) as Divine Mercy Sunday.

The liberating power of the sacrament

For his part Benedict XVI repeatedly called for a "rediscovery" of the sacrament of confession. At his homily in Washington on 17th April 2008, Pope Benedict affirmed: "The liberating power of this sacrament, in which our honest confession of sin is met by God's merciful word of pardon and peace, needs to be rediscovered and re-appropriated by every Catholic".

Pope Francis's preaching on the merciful love of God and his decision to have an Extraordinary Jubilee of Mercy

(8th December 2015 - 20th November 2016) can be seen in the context of the efforts of recent popes to draw the faithful to receive the forgiveness of sins in the sacrament of confession.

Take a fresh look at confession

In the Bull for the Indiction of the Extraordinary Jubilee of Mercy, Pope Francis launched the appeal: "Let us place the Sacrament of Reconciliation at the centre once more in such a way that it will enable people to touch the grandeur of God's mercy with their own hands".[3] These words are an invitation to look on the sacrament of confession with new eyes.

It makes sense to look at the Sacrament of Reconciliation with a renewed openness, because it is precisely this sacrament which brings about a profound renewal in us once and again on our journey towards God. "After confession we are reborn", as Francis explained at a Lenten Penitential Service in Rome.[4] When we reflect, we become aware of our need to be purified continuously along the road to holiness and eternal life. We do not want to become old in spirit or hardened in sin, and "through forgiveness the heart is renewed and rejuvenated".[5] Along with Anointing of the Sick, confession is a "sacrament of healing" though which Christ willed that his Church should continue his work of salvation here and now.[6]

THE MERCY OF GOD

God, all-powerful above all in his mercy

To understand and appreciate the Sacrament of Reconciliation we must look firstly to God. As a sacrament, confession is a divine action, and what is most important therefore is the silent but real activity of God the Father, Son and Holy Spirit in this rite. Before addressing our questions about confession it is helpful to consider God's view of and action in this sacrament. What does God do in this sacrament? What is the Lord's intention in our regard when we go to confession? Our minds and hearts are best illuminated by considering the mind and heart of Christ in regard to forgiveness and mercy.

The Opening Prayer (or Collect) of the 26th Sunday in Ordinary Time addresses God in the following way: "O God who manifest your almighty power above all by pardoning and showing mercy…" At first glance this phrase might surprise us. We might think that surely God shows he is all-powerful in creation, in bringing all that exists into being out of nothing. Or we might say that God shows his might above all in the Incarnation, by becoming man in Jesus Christ, or, indeed, in the miracles performed by our Lord.

Yet the faith of the Church expressed here in the liturgy professes that God shows his omnipotence above all in having mercy and forgiving. What can this mean? The forgiveness of sins brings about, constitutes, a new creation. The creation of all things from nothing does indeed show God's almighty power. But the "new creation" or "re-creation" by which we are transformed by grace into being beloved children of God and "partakers of the divine nature" (*2 P* 1:4) manifests God's omnipotence even more. St Paul teaches that through baptism we become a "new creation" (*2 Co* 5:17). From being sinners, we truly become beloved children of God, not just in name, but in reality (cf. *1 Jn* 3:1). The purification from sin which God carries out in confession effects our re-creation in Christ, and renews or reaffirms our divine filiation, that is, our identity as children of God in Christ which we received in baptism. Indeed St Gregory Nazianzen referred to penance as "the second baptism, the baptism of tears". In confession the Lord exercises his almighty power and love. This is the greatness of this sacrament, which transcends what we can fully understand and exceeds our greatest hopes and desires. In fact we can easily underestimate the beauty and power of this sacrament.

A God who continually forgives

St Josemaría Escrivá, a tireless apostle of the confessional, marvelled at the all-powerful love of God: "If God's power is marvellous in creating all things from nothing, if God is worthy of all love since out of love he redeems us on the cross, a God who continually forgives is more loving than all the mothers and fathers of this world put together".

The sacrament of forgiveness leads us then to know more deeply who God is. In the Bull *Misericordiae Vultus* ("The Face of Mercy") Pope Francis comments on this Collect prayer and cites the words of St Thomas Aquinas: "It is proper to God to exercise mercy, and he manifests his omnipotence particularly in this way".[7] These words of St Thomas, says the Holy Father, "show that God's mercy, rather than a sign of weakness, is the mark of his omnipotence… Throughout the history of humanity, God will always be the One who is present, close, provident, holy and merciful".[8]

"When God forgives he forgets"[9]

The Holy Father explains the mercy of God with particular reference to Sacred Scripture. Here it is God himself who proclaims his infinite patience and love. The Psalms are full of this teaching: "He forgives all your iniquity, he heals all your diseases, he redeems your life from the pit; he crowns you with steadfast love and mercy" (*Ps* 103:3-4; cf. *Ps* 146:7-9; 147:3.6). Psalm 136, cherished by the people of Israel as the "Great Hallel" has as its refrain: "For his mercy endures forever". Micah ends his prophecy with a sure affirmation of God's mercy: "He will again have compassion upon us, he will tread our iniquities under foot. You will cast all our sins into the depths of the sea" (7:19).

The hopes of the Old Testament for a Messiah, the saviour who would save his people from their sins, finds fulfilment in Jesus Christ. In his beautiful canticle, the Benedictus, Zechariah celebrates the coming of the Redeemer when he speaks of "the tender mercy of our God" which has dawned on his people from on high (*Lk* 1:78). Indeed, Christ is mercy incarnate. "With our eyes fixed on Jesus and his merciful gaze, we experience the love of the Most Holy Trinity".[10]

It is not easy for us to grasp or understand this limitless mercy of God who forgives and forgets, because we find it so hard to do this ourselves. Divine justice is very different to human justice.

Often we need images or metaphors to convey something of the reality of God's readiness to forgive the contrite sinner. Blessed Columba Marmion wrote that "we are infinitely rich in Jesus Christ and, compared with our miseries, the mercy of God is like an ocean compared to a drop of water".

God the Father of Mercies

The forgiveness of sins in confession is an action of the Blessed Trinity: Father, Son and Holy Spirit. While all God's actions outside of himself (*ad extra* actions) are one common action of the three divine persons, as the *Catechism of the Catholic Church* points out, "each divine person performs the common work according to his unique personal property" (n. 258).

The immense mercy of God the Father is best explained to us by Jesus himself in the beautiful parable of the prodigal son. The younger of two sons, who has gone and squandered his share of his father's hard-earned life's savings "in loose living" (*Lk* 15:13), only comes to his senses when famine reduces him to extreme poverty. He decides to return to his father's house to overcome his hunger: "How many of my father's hired servants have bread enough and to spare, but I perish here with hunger!" (*Lk* 15:17)

While there may not be clear signs of remorse on the part of the wayward son, there is no doubt at all as to the attitude of his father. It is worth reflecting on each of the five verbs contained in the description of the welcome the son receives from his father: "While he was yet at a distance, his father *saw* him and *had compassion*, and *ran* and *embraced* him and *kissed* him" (*Lk* 15:20). Christ leaves us in no doubt as to the attitude of God the Father to us sinners. The Father was eagerly awaiting his son and he spots him from a distance. He does not charge his son with the real injustice he has done to him. He takes the opening the son has given him to forgive and reinstate his son with great tenderness and joy.

Francis encourages the young people of the world towards confession with words that are like a commentary on this parable:

> God is there before us, always looking for us, and he finds us first. Maybe one of you feels something weighing on your heart. You are thinking: "I did this, I did that..." Do not be afraid! God is waiting for you! God is a father and he is always waiting for us! It is so wonderful to feel the merciful embrace of the Father in the Sacrament of Reconciliation, to discover that the confessional is a place of mercy.[11]

Jesus Christ, merciful Redeemer

God the Father sent us his Son to free us from sin. "For God so loved the world that he gave his only Son, that whoever believes in him should not perish but have eternal life" (*Jn* 3:16). This saving love of God is seen above all on the cross where Christ makes peace between heaven and earth by the shedding of his blood (cf. *Col* 1:20). Jesus is the Suffering Servant described so poignantly by the prophet Isaiah: "He was wounded for our transgressions, he was bruised for our iniquities; upon him was the chastisement that made us whole, and with his stripes we are healed" (*Is* 53:5).

A good stimulus and preparation for confession can be the contemplation of a crucifix, since the cross of Christ is the maximum expression of God's self-sacrificing love for sinners. Indeed, as the Holy Father puts it: "Jesus Christ is the face of the Father's mercy".[12]

The Holy Spirit, protagonist in the sacrament of mercy

On the evening of Easter Sunday, the day of his Resurrection, the Lord Jesus came to where his disciples were gathered. He "stood among them and said to them, 'Peace be with you'. When he had said this, he showed them his hands and his side" (*Jn* 20:19-20). The disciples are overcome with joy on realising that the Lord is truly risen from the dead. Then Christ gives them their mission: "Jesus said to them again, 'Peace be with you. As the Father has sent me, even so I send you.' And when he had said this, he breathed on them, and said to them, 'Receive the Holy Spirit. If you forgive the sins of any, they are forgiven; if you retain the sins of any, they are retained'" (*Jn* 20:21-23). Thus Christ entrusted to the priests of his Church the power to remit sins.

On the evening of his Resurrection, Christ shows his wounds to the disciples, and then breathing on them and giving the Holy Spirit, he confers on them "the ministry of reconciliation" (*2 Co* 5:18) to be exercised in the Church until the end of time. Pope Francis comments on this event: "Jesus reveals the wounds in his hands and side: these wounds represent the price of our salvation. The Holy Spirit brings us pardon 'by passing through' Jesus's wounds".[13]

The work of the Holy Spirit

The forgiveness of sins in confession is not a human act; it is the work of the Holy Spirit. In his catechesis on the Creed during the Year of Faith, the Holy Father dedicated an audience to our faith in "the remission of sins". Here he stated, "first of all, we must remember that *the principal agent in the forgiveness of sins is the Holy Spirit*".[14] In a similar vein, while addressing priests who were doing a course on the sacrament of penance, the Pope reminded them in the first place that *"the protagonist of the ministry of reconciliation is the Holy Spirit"*.[15]

In seeking to look at confession "from God's perspective" as it were, we are led to conclude with Pope Francis that the word "'mercy'…reveals the very mystery of the Most Holy Trinity". The forgiveness of our sins carried out in sacramental penance is a common work of all three divine persons of the Blessed Trinity. Indeed, the formula of absolution, which is pronounced by the priest in confession and which effects the forgiveness of sins, expresses very well the action of the Triune God in this sacrament, through the ministry of his Church:

> God the Father of mercies, through the death and Resurrection of his Son has reconciled the world to himself and sent the Holy Spirit among us for the forgiveness of sins; through the ministry of the Church, may God give you pardon and peace, and I absolve you

from your sins in the name of the Father, and of the Son, and of the Holy Spirit.

The joy of God in forgiving

We could not finish this attempt to consider confession "from God's point of view", without reflecting on how God rejoices in forgiving his children.

In his commentary on the account of the creation of the world in Genesis, St Ambrose drew attention to the fact that God rested on the seventh day, only after he had brought human beings into existence:

> Thanks, then, to the Lord our God who accomplished a work in which he might find rest. He made the heavens, but I do not read that he found rest there; he made the stars, the moon, the sun, and neither do I read that he found rest in them. I read instead that he made man and that then he rested, finding in man one to whom he could offer the forgiveness of sins.[16]

In the great parables of God's mercy in Chapter Fifteen of St Luke's Gospel, we find the same joy of God in forgiving sinners. In telling these stories, Christ is at pains to help us grasp the immense happiness of God in pardoning our sins. Thus the father of the prodigal son organises a great feast to "make merry" for this son who "was dead, and is alive again" (*Lk* 15:24).

The Shepherd

The unique value of each soul to God is also borne out by the image of the shepherd who loses one of his hundred sheep. He leaves the ninety-nine in the wilderness to go after the lost sheep. And very significantly, "when he has found it, he lays it on his shoulders, rejoicing. And when he comes home, he calls together his neighbours, saying to them: 'Rejoice with me, for I have found my sheep which was lost'" (*Lk* 15:5-6). Similarly, the woman who had lost one of her ten silver coins and seeks diligently until she finds it, invites her neighbours to celebrate with her. Our Lord comments on this festivity by saying: "Just so, I tell you, there is joy before the angels of God over one sinner who repents" (*Lk* 15:10).

Our reception of the sacrament of penance brings joy to the heart of God. Francis concluded a catechesis on this sacrament by urging the faithful:

Celebrating the Sacrament of Reconciliation means being enfolded in a warm embrace: it is the embrace of the Father's infinite mercy... I am telling you: each time we go to confession, God embraces us. God rejoices! Let us go forward on this road.[17]

GOING TO CONFESSION

Why we need confession

The Lord's mercy is inexhaustible, for those who seek forgiveness. God respects our freedom; we must freely ask for his pardon of our sins. "God who created you without you, will not save you without you", says St Augustine. Divine grace and human freedom work together for the salvation of our souls. God the Father "doesn't just leave the door open to us, but he awaits us", says Francis. "He is engaged in waiting for his children".[18] It is up to us to decide to enter the door of God's mercy.

Why do we need confession? We are called, each and every one of us, to be saints. In baptism we receive the new life of God, the life of holiness, symbolised in the white baptismal garment. However, due to the weakness of our fallen nature we are prone to sin and indeed we do fall along our journey towards heaven. This is why the Holy Father teaches that "conversion is not the question of a moment or a time of the year, it is an undertaking that lasts one's entire lifetime".[19] Indeed, "this is our life: to rise again continuously and resume our journey".[20]

Restoring friendship with God

At times it is more urgent to receive this sacrament, specifically, if one has committed a mortal sin. This is a sin "whose object is grave matter and which is committed with full knowledge and deliberate consent".[21] Because this sin means the loss of grace, the extinguishing of the divine life in us, the sooner we receive God's mercy and restore our friendship with him the better.

In any event, the Sacrament of Reconciliation is immensely fruitful since it gives us the opportunity to say sorry to God who has given us everything and proven his love in a supreme way on the cross. "God has shown his love for us in that while we were yet sinners Christ died for us" (*Rm* 5:8). We know how important it is for us in human relationships to be able to say sorry to those we have hurt or wronged in any way. The closer the person is to us, a parent, a sibling, a dear friend, the deeper our sorrow. In order to express our sorrow to our most loving friend of all, Jesus Christ, and to receive his forgiveness, we have the sacrament of confession.

While conversion is a free human choice, it is before all else a gift of God. Preaching in St Peter's Basilica to a large congregation of people about to go to confession, Pope Francis pointed out to them that "being here to experience his love, in any case, is above all a fruit of his grace… The power to confess our sins is a gift from God, it is a gift, it is 'his work'" (cf. *Ep* 2:8-10).[22] Thus, when we find it hard to go to confession, we do well to ask the Lord for the grace we need to approach this sacrament. In a special way, we might appeal to Mary, the Mother of Mercy, to lead us to her Son, to encourage us, as she did at Cana, to do whatever he tells us (cf. *Jn* 2:5).

Sorrow for our sins

We have already given some consideration to God's action in this sacrament. The Lord lovingly welcomes us and guides us, and most importantly of all grants us his healing and pardon in the words of absolution which the priest pronounces in the person of Christ. What is the part of the penitent, of the one who goes to confession? The *Catechism of the Catholic Church* clearly explains the three "acts of the penitent", namely contrition, the confession of sins, and satisfaction (nn. 1450-1459).

Among the penitent's acts, "contrition" or sorrow for sin occupies the first place. This contrition is called "perfect" if it arises from a love by which God is loved above all else, and "imperfect" (also called "attrition") if it arises from the consideration of sin's ugliness or the fear of eternal damnation and the other penalties threatening the sinner (contrition of fear). While we should aim to love God above all else and hence have perfect contrition, imperfect contrition is also a gift from God and is brought to completion by sacramental absolution in confession. Indeed the fact of approaching the sacrament of penance is already an expression of sorrow for sin. Our sorrow for sin includes "purpose of amendment" or the resolution not to sin again. This often has very practical implications such as the avoidance of "occasions of sin", namely places or situations that tend to lead to sin.

No one can be excluded

At times some people may consider that their particular sins cannot be forgiven, perhaps because they seem too serious and beyond pardon, or perhaps because of having been away from confession for a long time. In his preaching Pope Francis has dealt with this temptation in a very encouraging way:

> No one can be excluded from the mercy of God... With how much love Jesus looks at us! With how much love he heals our sinful heart! Our sins never scare him. Let us consider the prodigal son who, when he decided to return to his father, considers making a speech, but the father doesn't let him speak. He embraces him (cf. *Lk* 15:17-24). This is the way Jesus is with us. *'Father, I have so many sins...'* - *'But he will be glad if you go: he will embrace you with such love! Don't be afraid'*... Do not forget that God *forgives all*, and *forgives always*. Let us never tire of asking forgiveness.[23]

The mercy of God is beyond what we can fully grasp. The Lord forgives us, not because we are worthy, but because he loves us freely and infinitely. As Benedict XVI once put it, "God loves us in a way that we might call 'obstinate' and enfolds us in his inexhaustible tenderness".[24]

The consideration of the immensity of God's love will help us to confess and to have confidence in his mercy. As St Teresa of Avila urges in Chapter Nineteen of the book of her *Life*:

> Let us trust in the goodness of God, which is greater than all the evil we can do. When, with full knowledge of ourselves, we desire to return to friendship with him, he remembers neither our ingratitude nor our misuse of the favours that he has granted us… Let them remember his words and consider what he has done to me, who wearied of offending his majesty before he ceased forgiving me. Never does he weary of giving and never can his mercies be exhausted: let us, then, not grow weary of receiving.

Sincere confession of our sins

The question is often asked: why the need to confess to a priest? Is it not sufficient to confess my sins to God privately in my own heart? There are many reasons why "confession to a priest is an essential part of the sacrament of penance".[25]

"First", as Francis explains, "the forgiveness of our sins is not something we can give ourselves. I cannot say: I forgive my sins. Forgiveness is asked for, is asked of another, and in confession we ask for forgiveness from Jesus. Forgiveness is not the fruit of our own efforts but rather a gift".[26]

Secondly, as we saw in Chapter Twenty of St John's Gospel, the risen Lord entrusted the mission and power to forgive sins to priests within his Church. The Church is the place where Christ continues his work of salvation here and now through the power of the Holy Spirit. "That is why it is not enough to ask the Lord for forgiveness in one's own mind and heart, but why instead it is necessary humbly and trustingly to confess one's sins to a minister of the Church".[27]

Moreover sins, even the most hidden ones, have an impact on others, especially on our brothers and sisters in the faith. An offence against God is also an offence against his people, and that is why pardon must be sought of the Church in the person of the priest, a sacred minister of the Church. The Holy Father has pointed out that the Sacrament of Reconciliation frees us from the tendency towards individualism and subjectivism. "God forgives every penitent sinner, personally, but the Christian is tied to Christ, and Christ is united to the Church".[28]

Advantages to confession

Besides these reasons there are very good human advantages to confessing our sins. The Lord has designed his sacraments wisely and lovingly, in a way that best responds to the needs of our nature. As the *Catechism* points out, "the confession (or disclosure) of sins, even from a simply human point of view, frees us, and facilitates our reconciliation with others"[29].

In a word, it is helpful psychologically and emotionally to be able to unburden ourselves. Moreover, the words of absolution which we hear in confession provide an external assurance of forgiveness which is very important for our inner peace. Because confession provides this objective confirmation of pardon, "we have to appreciate it" says Francis. "It is a gift, a cure, a protection as well as the assurance that God has forgiven me"[30].

It may also be added that the honest confession of our sins is a powerful antidote to superficiality. Freely to recognise, articulate and own up to what we have done badly stretches us in a healthy way that helps us to grow and mature as people.

Sincerity

Of course the confession of our sins requires us to be sincere. It is the teaching of the Church, as expressed at the Council of Trent that "all mortal sins of which penitents after a diligent self-examination are conscious must be recounted by them in confession, even if they are most secret"[31]. If we wish to receive pardon for offences committed, it makes sense to ask forgiveness for each of those offences. This is why it is helpful to examine our consciences before going to confession so as to confess our sins as best as we can remember.[32] It is good to be simple, straightforward and to the point. As Friar Laurence says to Romeo in Shakespeare's *Romeo and Juliet*: "Be plain good son and homely in thy drift, Riddling confession finds but riddling shrift" (Act II, Scene 3)[33].

We may well have to battle against feelings of shame. After all, no one enjoys saying what he or she has done wrong, and some sins cause us greater embarrassment. The Holy Father has addressed this all-too-human challenge on several occasions in his characteristically direct style. "*'But Father, I am ashamed...'* Shame is also good; it is healthy to feel a little shame, because being ashamed is salutary... Shame too does good, because it makes us more humble".[34] The sacrament of confession does not humiliate us, but it does humble us, and humility is the path to holiness.

The honest confession of our sins helps us to be simple, less complicated internally, and hence more serene. In his *Treatise on Penance*, St Ambrose wrote: "If you want to be justified, confess your fault: a humble confession of faults untangles the knot of faults".

The need to make reparation

The third act of the penitent is "satisfaction", the need to make up for our sins in so far as we can.[35] As Pope Francis explains in his Bull for the Year of Mercy, "God goes beyond justice with his mercy and forgiveness.

Yet this does not mean that justice should be devalued or rendered superfluous. On the contrary: anyone who makes a mistake must pay the price".[36] Making reparation is not a question of trying to satisfy an implacable God, but rather a requirement of justice, of love of God and of our human nature. As the Pope told a large gathering of priests: "Mercy…does not exclude but rather includes the just obligation to atone for, to the extent possible, the wrong committed".[37]

An act of love

Atonement is an act of love which seeks to reunite us fully with God who is the fulness of Love. Further, while absolution takes away sin it does not remove all the disorders caused by sin. "In the Sacrament of Reconciliation God forgives our sins which he truly blots out; and yet sin leaves a negative effect on the way we think and act".[38] Human freedom and dignity also demand that we have the opportunity to make up for our sins and faults freely and lovingly.

The need to do penance in order to expiate the "temporal punishment due to sin" is part of the sacrament of confession. This is why the confessor assigns a particular penance to the penitent. Besides this, we can always offer other penances in the course of our daily lives through which we make a loving reparation to God and by which Christ is formed ever more fully in us (cf. *Ga* 4:19).

The value of frequent confession

The *Compendium of the Catechism of the Catholic Church* offers a useful summary of the effects of the sacrament of penance:

> reconciliation with God and therefore the forgiveness of sins; reconciliation with the Church; recovery, if it has been lost, of the state of grace; remission of the eternal punishment due to mortal sins, and remission, at least in part, of the temporal punishment which is the consequence of sin; peace, serenity of conscience and spiritual consolation; and an increase of spiritual strength for the struggle of Christian living (n. 310).

This list, which contains much of what we have seen in the preaching of Francis, also provides the rationale for frequent confession. This sacrament is a source of immense grace, ongoing purification and increasing intimacy with God. Not only are our sins forgiven but we receive the spiritual strength we need to keep up the Christian battle by growing in the virtues. Moreover confession can often be a setting in which to receive spiritual direction.

Our sins are always the same

We may sometimes be bothered by the thought that our sins are always the same. Benedict XVI addressed this concern very effectively in a catechesis to thousands of First Holy Communion children:

It is very helpful to confess with a certain regularity. It is true: our sins are always the same, but we clean our homes, our rooms, at least once a week, even if the dirt is always the same; in order to live in cleanliness, in order to start again. Otherwise, the dirt might not be seen but it builds up. Something similar can be said about the soul, for me myself: if I never go to confession, my soul is neglected and in the end I am always pleased with myself and no longer understand that I must work hard to improve, that I must make progress. And this cleansing of the soul which Jesus gives us in the sacrament of confession helps us to make our consciences more alert, more open, and hence, it also helps us to mature spiritually and as human person... It is very helpful to confess regularly in order to foster the cleanliness and beauty of the soul and to mature day by day in life.[39]

Growing in charity

While confession nurtures our faith and hope, above all it is an effective means to grow in charity, the greatest of all the virtues (cf. *1 Co* 13). The scene of the sinful woman who comes up to the Lord at the feast in the house of Simon the Pharisee is striking and also instructive. Standing behind Christ "at his feet, weeping, she began to wet his feet with her tears and wiped them with the hair of her head, and kissed his feet, and anointed them with ointment" (*Lk* 7:38). To those who were scandalised by her actions, Christ firmly replied: "I tell you, her sins, which are many, are forgiven, for she loved much; but he who is forgiven little, loves little" (*Lk* 7:47).

This poor woman had reverenced Christ's body in advance of the Passion in which the Lord's body would be broken and his blood would flow to redeem the world from sin. By her actions she showed a deep contrition and loving refinement - she made reparation in advance for the crucifixion of Jesus - which God abundantly blessed by granting her forgiveness of all her sins.

Being open to the mercy of God increases our charity, while in turn our love of God will lead us to seek his pardon often.

Being Instruments of God's Mercy

Helping others towards confession

St Luke recounts that one day our Lord was teaching in a very crowded house. Meanwhile some men came along "bringing on a bed a man who was paralyzed and they sought to bring him in and lay him before Jesus; but finding no way to bring him in because of the crowd, they went up on the roof and let him down with his bed through the tiles into the midst before Jesus" (*Lk* 5:18-19). We can only imagine the reaction of Christ's listeners as the man's stretcher was carefully lowered down to the ground before him. When the Lord "saw their faith he said: 'Man, your sins are forgiven you'" (*Lk* 5:20).

The Lord frees this man from his sins, and then from his physical paralysis thanks to the daring faith of his friends. With great determination they had set about presenting their needy friend to Christ the Healer. By virtue of our baptism, we are all apostles of Christ, with the duty and the capacity to be instruments to help one another come closer to God. Notwithstanding the fact that we are sinners ourselves, we can seek to help others receive the mercy of God by promoting the sacrament of confession. We are rightly concerned for the material needs of others; how should we be any less concerned for their spiritual needs, which can have an eternal significance?

The example of our own commitment

Words of encouragement or an explanation of the sacrament can help, and above all the example of our own commitment to sacramental penance. In fact, as Pope Francis has pointed out, "so many people, including young people, are returning to the Sacrament of Reconciliation".[40] Young people can often bring one another to confession; parents can give example to their children; one friend can encourage another; priests and teachers can explain the greatness of this sacrament.

After freeing the demoniac in the country of the Gerasenes, Jesus entrusted him with this mission: "Go home to your friends, and tell them how much the Lord has done for you, and how he has had mercy on you" (*Mk* 5:19). Throughout the Gospel, those who receive the mercy of God naturally seek to spread that good news. Thus the Samaritan woman, after her saving conversation with Christ at the well, "left her water jar, and went away into the city, and said to the people, 'Come see a man who told me all that I ever did'" (*Jn* 4:28-29).

The words of Pope Francis are a strong encouragement to this apostolate of confession. Addressing university students gathered in St Peter's Basilica during Lent to go to confession, the Holy Father charged them with bringing the news of reconciliation to the people around them:

> To the many you will meet, you can communicate the joy of receiving the forgiveness of the Father and of rediscovering full friendship with him. And you will tell them that our Father awaits us, our Father forgives, and furthermore that he rejoices. If you go to him with your whole life, even with the many sins, instead of reproaching you, he will rejoice: this is our Father. This you must say, say it to many people, today… Let us receive mercy, and let us give mercy![41]

Priests and penance

As ministers of confession, priests can encourage the reception of this sacrament in specific ways.

In the first place priests need to receive this sacrament regularly themselves. "We become good confessors when, above all, we allow ourselves to be penitents in search of his mercy", Francis reminds priests.[42] For his part, St John Paul II issued a serious and helpful warning in his Apostolic Exhortation on *Reconciliation and Penance*:

> The priest's celebration of the Eucharist and administration of other sacraments, his pastoral zeal, his relationship with the faithful, his communion with his brother priests, his collaboration with his bishop,

his life of prayer - in a word, the whole of his priestly existence, suffers an inexorable decline if by negligence or for some other reason he fails to receive the sacrament of penance at regular intervals and in a spirit of genuine faith and devotion. If a priest were no longer to go to confession or properly confess his sins, his priestly being and his priestly action would feel its effects very soon, and this would be noticed by the community of which he was the pastor.[43]

Model confessors

Priests can effectively promote confession also by their availability to administer this sacrament. When there is a regular and generous time for confessions the fruits are not slow in coming. During his pontificate Benedict XVI proposed several saintly priests as models for confessors, including St John Mary Vianney, St Pius of Pietrelcina (Padre Pio), St Joseph Cafasso and St Josemaría Escrivá. Pope Francis decided that the remains of Padre Pio would be venerated in St Peter's Basilica in February 2016, during the Year of Mercy. Following the example of these holy confessors, priests can also promote Reconciliation by the preaching and catechesis they give on this sacrament.

Moreover priests themselves derive great spiritual benefit from administering this sacrament. The priest's fundamental identity as *alter Christus* - "another Christ" - is reinforced by exercising the ministry of reconciliation.

His faith can be strengthened by witnessing the faith of so many good people who confess. His understanding of the Mass as the saving sacrifice of the cross is made clearer in light of the remission of sins in virtue of Christ's Passion.

The personal witness of Pope Francis

In his catechesis on confession the Holy Father has spoken of his own reception of the sacrament: "Even the Pope confesses every fortnight, because the Pope is also a sinner".[44]

Moreover he has told how the discovery of his vocation is linked with this sacrament. In his Message for World Youth Day 2016 he recounted: "When I was seventeen years old, it happened one day that, as I was about to go out with friends, I decided to stop into a church first. I met a priest there who inspired great confidence, and I felt the desire to open my heart in confession. That meeting changed my life!"

Biographers of the Pope state that the date of that confession was 21st September, the feast of St Matthew. In his Bull on the Year of Mercy, Francis writes that

the calling of Matthew is presented within the context of mercy. Passing by the tax-collector's booth, Jesus looked intently at Matthew. It was a look full of mercy that forgave the sins of that man, a sinner and a tax collector… St Bede the Venerable, commenting on this

Gospel passage, wrote that Jesus looked upon Matthew
with merciful love and chose him: *miserando atque
eligendo.* This expression impressed me so much that I
chose it for my episcopal motto.[45]

The Holy Father's preaching on confession contains a
strong element of personal witness. This may help us also
in our apostolate of confession to encourage others by
example and to speak simply about the help we receive
from this sacrament. The fact that the Pope links his
vocation with this sacrament is also a reminder of how
many vocations of all kinds are discerned, strengthened
and sustained by frequent reception of the sacrament of
mercy.

Our Lady, Mother of Mercy

Loving mothers always seek to bring their children together
and to heal any division that may have arisen among them.
This is supremely the case with Our Lady. She collaborates
in a unique way in her Son's mission of reconciling the
world to God (cf. *2 Co* 5:19). For this reason we can be
sure that she intercedes for us in a particular way as we
seek the Lord's forgiveness in confession. We can make
the Holy Father's prayer our own:

"May the sweetness of her countenance watch over
us, so that all of us may rediscover the joy of God's
tenderness".[46]

Endnotes

[1] Francis, Audience, 19th February 2014.

[2] Francis, Homily [Parish of St Anne in the Vatican], 17th March 2013.

[3] Francis, Bull of Indiction of the Extraordinary Jubilee of Mercy, *Misericordiae Vultus*, 11th April [Divine Mercy Sunday] 2015, 17.

[4] Francis, Homily, Celebration of Penance. Communal Reconciliation Service with Individual Confession and Absolution, Vatican Basilica, 13th March 2015.

[5] Francis, Homily, Celebration of Penance. Communal Reconciliation Service with Individual Confession and Absolution, Vatican Basilica, 28th March 2014.

[6] Cf. *Catechism of the Catholic Church* 1421.

[7] St Thomas Aquinas, *Summa Theologiae*, II-II, q. 30, a. 3.

[8] Francis, Bull of Indiction of the Extraordinary Jubilee of Mercy, *Misericordiae Vultus*, 11th April [Divine Mercy Sunday], 2015, 6.

[9] Francis, Homily, Celebration of Penance. Communal Reconciliation Service with Individual Confession and Absolution, 13th March 2015.

[10] Francis, Bull of Indiction of the Extraordinary Jubilee of Mercy, *Misericordiae Vultus*, 11th April [Divine Mercy Sunday] 2015, 8.

[11] Francis, Message for World Youth Day 2016, 15th August, 2015, 2.

[12] Francis, Bull of Indiction of the Extraordinary Jubilee of Mercy, *Misericordiae Vultus*, 11th April [Divine Mercy Sunday] 2015, 1.

[13] Francis, Audience, 20th November 2013.

[14] Francis, Audience, 20th November 2013.

[15] Francis, Address, 28th March 2014.

[16] St Ambrose, *Hexameron*, 6, 10, 76. This text of St Ambrose is commented on by St John Paul II in *Dies Domini*, his Apostolic Letter on keeping the Lord's Day holy, 31st May 1998, 61.

[17] Francis, Audience, 19th February 2014.

[18] Francis, Homily, Celebration of Penance. Communal Reconciliation

Service with Individual Confession and Absolution, 28th March 2014.

[19] Francis, Homily, Celebration of Penance. Communal Reconciliation Service with Individual Confession and Absolution, 28th March 2014.

[20] Francis, Audience, 20th November 2013.

[21] *Catechism of the Catholic Church* 1857.

[22] Francis, Homily, Celebration of Penance. Communal Reconciliation Service with Individual Confession and Absolution, 13th March 2015.

[23] Francis, Homily, Celebration of Penance. Communal Reconciliation Service with Individual Confession and Absolution, 13th March 2015.

[24] Benedict XVI, Homily at the Parish of God the Merciful Father, Rome, 26th March 2006.

[25] *Catechism of the Catholic Church* 1456.

[26] Francis, Audience, 19th February 2014, 1.

[27] Francis, Audience, 19th February 2014, 2.

[28] Francis, Audience, 20th November 2013.

[29] *Catechism of the Catholic Church* 1455.

[30] Francis, Audience, 20th November 2013.

[31] Council of Trent (1551); cf. *Catechism of the Catholic Church* 1456.

[32] On examination of conscience before confession, cf. *Catechism of the Catholic Church* 1454.

[33] "Shrift" is an old world for the sacrament of confession.

[34] Francis, Audience, 19th February 2014, 2.

[35] Cf. *Catechism of the Catholic Church* 1459-1467.

[36] Francis, Bull of Indiction of the Extraordinary Jubilee of Mercy, *Misericordiae Vultus*, 11th April [Divine Mercy Sunday] 2015, 21.

[37] Francis, Address, 12th March 2015.

[38] Francis, Bull of Indiction of the Extraordinary Jubilee of Mercy, *Misericordiae Vultus*, 11th April [Divine Mercy Sunday] 2015, 22.

[39] Benedict XVI, catechetical meeting with children who had received First Holy Communion during the year, 15th October 2005.

[40] Francis, Bull of Indiction of the Extraordinary Jubilee of Mercy, *Misericordiae Vultus*, 11th April [Divine Mercy Sunday], 2015, 17.

[41] Francis, Homily, Celebration of Penance. Communal Reconciliation Service with Individual Confession and Absolution, 28th March 2014.

[42] Francis, Bull of Indiction of the Extraordinary Jubilee of Mercy, *Misericordiae Vultus*, 11th April [Divine Mercy Sunday] 2015, 17.

[43] St John Paul II, Apostolic Exhortation *Reconciliatio et Paenitentia*, 2nd December 1984 31, VI.

[44] Francis, Audience, 20th November 2013.

[45] Francis, Bull of Indiction of the Extraordinary Jubilee of Mercy, *Misericordiae Vultus*, 11th April [Divine Mercy Sunday] 2015, 8.

[46] Francis, Bull of Indiction of the Extraordinary Jubilee of Mercy, *Misericordiae Vultus*, 11th April [Divine Mercy Sunday] 2015, 24.

Images

Page 7: *Christ at the Pool of Bethesda*, 1667-70 (oil on canvas), Murillo, Bartolome Esteban (1618-82) / National Gallery, London, UK / Bridgeman Images.

Page 18: *The Good Shepherd* (oil on canvas), Champaigne, Philippe de (1602-74) / Musee des Beaux-Arts, Lille, France / Bridgeman Images.

Page 37: *Madonna and Child*, 1650 - 1655 (oil on canvas), Murillo, Bartolome Esteban (1618-82) / Palazzo Pitti, Florence, Italy / Mondadori Portfolio/Electa/Sergio Anelli / Bridgeman Images.